P9-CKU-712

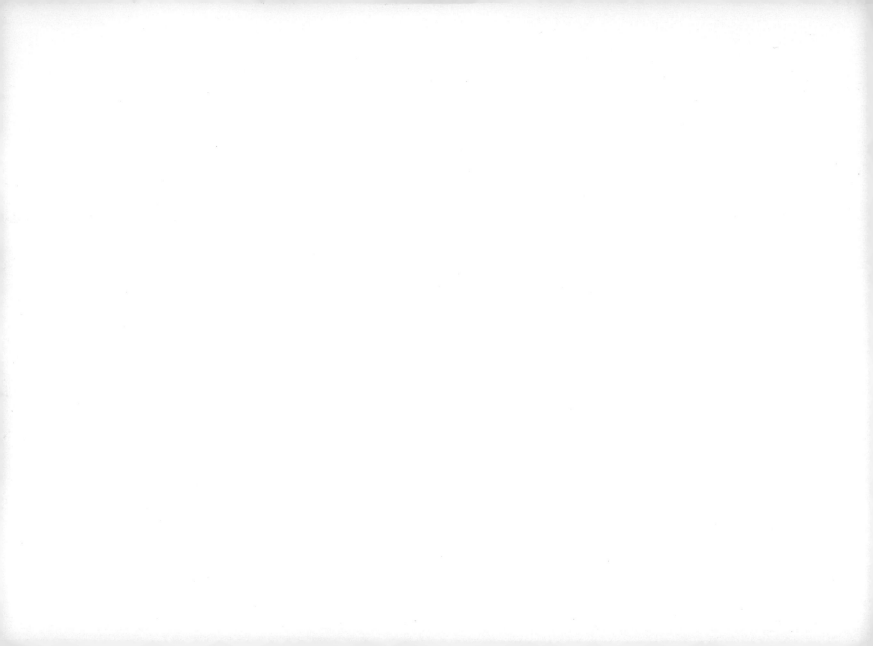

Dordogne

Portraits of France©

Photos Denis Nidos and Bernard Dupuy
Original text Suzanne Boireau-Tartarat
Translation Jacqui Taylor

Editorial direction Bertrand Dalin

Many thanks to all who contributed to this publication,
especially to Claire Delbos, Dominique Lavigne and Joëlle Chevé,
and to the Semitour.

*Cover picture - Flock of geese. The Dordogne
owes its international gastronomic reputation
to these webbed-footed creatures' foies gras.*

*Previous page - The Dordogne is an endless series
of perspectives; green hills rising up into blue sky,
like here, at the Château de Montbazillac.*

Summary

Previous page - The Dordogne, land of contrasts,
finds harmony in a play of shapes and colours.

In the villages, swathes of green cover
and take over the old stone walls

Editorial

There are still spectacular traces of human history to be found in the Dordogne. Cave paintings at Lascaux or de Villars; fortified towns, abbeys and castles of all periods and all styles. With so many villages of character where time seems to have stood still, this is truly an uncommon heritage.

The countryside is just as varied and appealing. Fields, lakes, forests, peaceful waterways winding sensuously through hilly landscapes where it is pleasant to wander.

A certain art of living is cultivated here, more so than elsewhere. The local products have a solid reputation: foie gras, truffles, chestnuts, walnuts, Monbazillac and Bergerac wines, to mention but a few...

Here, then, is the colourful Dordogne, let loose in words and pictures!

Previous page - In the Dordogne, architecture and nature blend into unforgettable sights, like the Château de Puyguilhem at Villars.

The fortified town or 'bastide' de Monpazier, typical of its kind, often serves as a film set.

History

In the beginning was the Dordogne, and well before its history, its prehistory. That science began here in the late XIXth century, as the great sites were waking up from their thousand-millennia-old sleep – sites which gave their names to prehistoric ages: Magdalenian, Mousterian, Gravettian, etc.

The prehistory scouts all came to the Vézère valley, looking for an explanation of our origins: the abbé Breuil, Leroi-Gourhan and Denis Peyrony tried to interpret the traces abandoned by our ancestors 32 000 years ago. The National Museum at Les Eyzies, where the finishing touches are currently being put to a large extension, provides the essential background knowledge for a visit to the caves and rock deposits. Font-de-Gaume, Rouffignac and so many others, notably Lascaux (17 000 B.C), closed since 1963 for conservation reasons, though a disturbing replica of the site makes up for this.

Previous page - Lascaux. The famous cave has been closed to the public since 1963, owing to an outbreak of microorganisms on the walls. The facsimile Lascaux II was opened in 1983 on the initiative of the Dordogne department, and arouses real emotion. (Photo © Semitour)

Earth draped in its natural lace at the Villars cave.

*Above and following page - The Cistercian abbey
at Boschaud drowsing in history like a mirage
in the Villars countryside. All that remain are parts
of the choir and transept, traces of the cloister
and the abbey buildings and bits of the
pendentive cupola.*

The Cussac cave at Buisson-de-Cadouin, most recent discovery to date, contains panels carved with 22 000 year-old animal figures and tracings, and the remains of human bones (it is closed to visitors).

Once Romanised, the Gallic Petrocore tribes set up the rich town of Vesunna, the ancestor of Périgueux. By the year 1000 and the end of the barbaric invasions, religion was asserting its power in the feudal world of the castles, and Romanesque churches and abbeys sprang up like stars in the firmament.

Eleanor was married to the future Plantagenet King of England Henry II in 1152, bringing him the duchy of Aquitaine in her dowry. The local lords wavered for a long time between Capetians and Plantagenets, as did the troubadour warrior Bertran de Born with Richard the Lionheart. The Dordogne was torn apart in this way until the battle of Castillon in 1453, which marked the end of a two-hundred-year conflict.

Feudal and religious power dominated medieval life.

*Left - Chancelade Abbey was a Mecca of intellectual life from the XII*th *century. A walk along the Beauronne riverbanks lets you to look at the whole place, together with the convent buildings.*

Centre - In the Middle Ages the slightest cliff became a stronghold. Here, the Château de Beynac.

Right - The Romanesque church Saint-Léon-sur-Vézère with its dazzlingly perfect proportions.

During these turbulent centuries wars followed hard upon epidemics – the Black Pest in 1348 – and famine, not forgetting the crusade against the Cathares led by Simon de Montfort in 1212. The villages were fortified, the walled towns appeared and the castles defended their positions as strongholds for one camp or the other.

It seems to be ruining castles of all periods and styles in the Dordogne.

Condensed history on the Commarque site, occupied from prehistoric times.

The Château des Milandes was owned by Josephine Baker and Jo Bouillon. A museum is devoted to the star of the Revue Negre.

1562 brought the Wars of Religion. Southern Dordogne, won over to the reformed religion, was particularly touched. There was a Jacquerie peasant revolt in 1595, then in 1637 when heavy taxes were levied to finance the war.

Peasant conditions remained difficult until the early XXth century. The first agricultural meetings were organised at Lanouaille by Marshal Bugeaud, who contributed to agricultural modernisation, and whose motto was 'by the plough and by the sword'.

Previous page - A town dominated by its castle in verdant countryside: this is the Dordogne's magic formula. Here, Salignac-Eyvigues.

Mareuil, once one of the four baronies of the Dordogne, and a rare example of a fortress built on the plain.

Like a dream between sky and water, the Château de Losse has always seemed to hesitate on its huge diving-board.

During the Second Empire the railway wiped out the inland water transport economy and gave birth to a working class, notably in Périgueux. The losses sustained in the wars of 1870 and — especially — 1914, and the drift from the land resulting from the economic crises of the second half of the XIXth century made deep black furrows in the demographic picture. State education was progressively implanted in the department, parents balking at losing such a convenient workforce. Little by little, local dialects gave way to French.

Many of the Dordogne's sons died for France in 1914. The department was also an enclave of Resistance in the Second World War.

Following page - The lives of certain peasants were still very hard in deepest Dordogne between the wars, though they were not necessarily like Jacquou le Croquant's.

However, the Félibrée festival embodies the Occitan spirit every year, celebrating rural traditions, troubadours and old-fashioned crafts. During the Second World War, the Dordogne took in thousands of refugees from Alsace and Lorraine. The Resistance 'maquis' was divided between Gaullist and communist forces. In this department won over to radicalism, politics is as popular a sport as rugby, and the Republican banquets have always been as much about debating ideas as convivial feasting.

The Dordogne department, created in 1790, established itself on the traditional characteristics of the Périgord region: this province has kept the same strong identity throughout its history, despite being drawn towards Limousin in the north, Quercy in the east, Guyennne in the south and Charente in the west.

Previous page - The Perigord Bournat keeps
up the regional language and Occitan tradition
which exult once a year at the Félibrée festival.
This is a folklore festival for some, a source
of indispensable memories for others,
but it attracts thousands of visitors with its
costumes, dances and old-fashioned crafts.

The Félibrée is held in a town in the Dordogne
on the first Sunday in July. Here, it is taking
place in Périgueux.

The Dordogne's great intellectuals have left their mark on the history of French thought: Fénelon, Brantôme, Montaigne, la Boétie, Lagrange-Chancel, Maine de Biran, Eugène le Roy, Léon Bloy, Elisée Reclus, André Maurois, Rachilde, Emile Goudeau, François Augiéras...as well as some more contemporary figures like Josephine Baker and Sylvain Floirat.

The Industrial Revolution left the Dordogne out: little by little, forges and watermills stopped running on the waterways, and the department was only split in two by its first motorway this very millennium. It is almost surprising to see a big stationery group at Condat on the Vézère, a few kilometres from Lascaux, as if, by some miracle, the local economy managed to reconcile industry and tourism.

Brantôme, author of Vies des dames galantes, *left his stamp on the Dordogne's intellectual life, as have so many other literary figures throughout history.*

Following page - Many watermills, formerly active, now converted into weekend homes, cling on to the Dordogne's rivers and waterways. Like here, at Bourdeilles, on the Dronne.

For if the Dordogne has missed several steps to modernity, owing chiefly to that hemmed-in position from which it is trying to escape, the department catches up in the field of tourism, putting to good use its historic wealth in an almost entirely natural and unspoiled landscape.

This environmental 'green gold' has allowed for the recent creation of a Périgord-Limousin natural park, in partnership with the bordering region.

Previous page - The flocks wander across a monochrome green spectrum, from the fluorescent prairie to the darker edges of the wood.

The countryside remains an agricultural space, even when open to tourism.

The leisure civilisation caters for trends as diverse as the call of the land, with 'green' tourism anchored in the rural world, and the taste for prestigious campsites and hotels. A wide range of sites, entertainment and leisure complexes suits all tastes. Cultural activities step up the pace during the summer season, with plenty of festivals: classical music, folklore, theatre, mime and jazz.

Above and following page - The Dordogne dips into its history and natural wealth to enrich the cultural and tourist heritage. At Sorgues (above), a truffle eco museum reveals the secrets of this 'black gold', while at Cendrieux (following page) descendants of the Emperor have opened a museum devoted to Napoleon where they organise historical reconstructions.

Agriculture is on the wane, and visibly so for those crops until recently dominant, such as tobacco, strawberries and apples, but it remains a strong economic basis for the logical development of other channels, notably duck and goose products and wood.

A network of small and medium-sized businesses and industries is very active in the leading-edge technology and farm-produce sectors, while those activities needing a large workforce, notably the footwear industry which has left its stamp on the Isle valley, are in decline. With slightly more than 400 000 inhabitants, the Dordogne attracts the newly-retired and back-to- the-land incomers who set up their business in the countryside to escape from the big cities.

Previous page - Rural life means a working day within a protected environment, like here, at Saint-Crépin and Carlucet in the Sarladais.

Breeding is still an important part of agriculture: cattle and sheep take advantage of the Dordogne's green prairies.

More and more foreign residents are settling in the Dordogne, especially the British community... Relations between the region and Britain go back a long way, but they were once much stormier. The British like the Ribéracois and the Bergeracois, perhaps because the green landscape seems familiar, with the warmer climate as an extra. They come on holiday and end up retiring here, participating more or less in local life.

Some European citizens start property businesses, or go in for tourism or wine-growing. Thanks to them, at least, whole hamlets have been completely renovated, and prices of rural property have shot up. A British newspaper, The News, is edited in Périgueux, there are flights between Bergerac and London and a cricket club at Eymet.

Rural architecture uses each region's own raw materials: ochre and phonolite in the Dordogne valley, cob in the Double, shale and slate in the Périgord highlands. Hamlets and villages blend into the landscape with the sheen of time on their stonework.

Secure in its history, the Dordogne can look forward to the future: heritage and space are not the least of assets when one's vocation is tourism. The aging population, which could be seen as a weakness, represents an economic mainspring in the health and social sectors, with the development of homecare services.

Employment is still dependent on the development of small units strongly reinforced by brainpower, but also on a more traditional network of craftsmen and small quality producers. Land of contrasts, heir to a rich past and open to new human adventures, the Dordogne is surely eternal.

Living and eating well are essential in the Dordogne: some good old-fashioned bread, and the meal is ready...

Following page - Nature plays with the elements, arching a halo of ephemeral magic over that eternal beauty.

Towns and Villages

Rural, and proud of it, the Dordogne is starred with villages often considered to be among the most beautiful in France. Time seems to have stood still since the Middle Ages in many of them — until the ringing of a mobile phone breaks the spell. These small villages perfumed with the countryside, however, must wait — honour where honour is due: the visit begins in the capital, situated right in the centre of the department.

Previous page - Saint-Front Cathedral stands out from its surroundings with its Byzantine curves, domes and pinnacles pointing to the sky as if wanting to prick divine curiosity.

A summer walk through the village stretches between brightness and shadow, fiery sun and refreshing darkness, in the light and shade of the alleyways.

Périgueux, town of art and history, was given a remarkable face-lift in the seventies through the impetus of the loi Malraux: the renovation campaign has barely finished in this vast protected sector, and the Perigourdins themselves are rediscovering their town as the first 'customers' of those guided and animated tours proposed by the tourist office, torch in hand and medieval buffet at the end of the day.

The town's origins are on the banks of the Isle. Near the Vésone tower, remains of an immense sanctuary, the Gallo-Roman museum designed by the architect Jean Nouvel retraces Vesunna's splendid past. This site museum, opened in July 2003, is transparent to create perspectives between the domus it is built on, the collections exhibited and the surrounding park. In the jardin des Arènes, walls from the antique amphitheatre have been preserved intact. This amphitheatre was demolished in the XIIth century. It could take up to 20,000 spectators.

You will soon be able to walk from one end of the agglomeration
to the other along the banks of the Isle. Whether on foot,
roller-skates or a bike, what a delight to rediscover
the town from the water's edge!

Following page - Vesunna, the Gallo-Roman museum built
on a domus, tells the story of public and private life in antiquity.
The transparent architecture is the work of Jean Nouvel.

This quarter of the town, organised around the Cité church and the Château Barrière, started to lose its influence as a commercial town grew up round the relics of Saint Front, honoured by pilgrims on the road to Compostella. Cité and Puy-Saint-Front joined up in 1240, and Périgueux was born. The church of Saint-Front became a cathedral in 1669, and was registered as a Way of Saint James site with the Unesco World Heritage in 1999. The building was reshaped in the XIXth century by Abadie, architect of the Sacré-Coeur in Montmartre, who took off the roof sheltering five domes and added twelve pinnacles, thus intensifying the Byzantine charm of a church built in the form of a Greek cross.

Previous page - Château Barrière, backing on to the remains of the late Empire wall. The façade is richly decorated in the Renaissance style.

Splendid Renaissance staircase in the Hôtel de la Joubertie, rue de la Sagesse, in Périgueux. It can only be visited as part of a guided tour, with the Tourist Office.

The Mataguerre tower is all that remains of the ramparts which enclosed the town until the XVIIIth century. They were demolished to open up access to the boulevards in the XIXth century. One of the oldest houses in Périgueux, les Dames de la Foy, can be found in the Mataguerre quarter.

From the Mataguerre tower there is a view right across Puy-Saint-Front to the cathedral.

Following page - The Tourist Office welcomes visitors near the Mataguerre tower,
last remains of the ramparts whose 28 towers and 12 doors protected the town.

Back to the Place Saint-Louis and the Limogeanne quarter, where the Renaissance transfigured the façades of the medieval alleys. The courtyards and house fronts of mansions visible from the street make this a particularly beautiful place to walk.

The guided tours organised by the Tourist Office allow you to visit the private staircases inside these mansions. This perimeter contains architectural treasures: the moulded porches, latticed windows and pilasters of the Maison du Pâtissier and the Méredieu, Crémoux, d'Estignard and Gamanson mansions are a feast for the eyes.

The Maison du Pâtissier (a reference to the pie-makers who supplied the French court, rather than to sweet pastry-makers) which dominates the Place Saint-Louis has 'postcard' charm.

Following page
Left - The chapter loft, a corbelled and half-timbered house, is a former ford lodge.

Right - The Saint-Front mansion, also called the Hôtel de Gamanson, is split into two buildings, leading off from a stair tower. The decorated façades overhang the main courtyard.

From the Freemasons' temple, whose façade is one of the most beautiful in France, slip down to the Pont de Barris. This bridge is the place to contemplate the banks of the River Isle and the three Renaissance mansions of the XVth, XVIth and XVIIth centuries, with their finely-worked skylights, galleries and sculpted colonnades, christened 'quay houses'.

The Hôtel de Fayolle overlooks the Isle above Amberg Square, marked out in honour of the German town twinned with Périgueux.

The XVIth century Lambert house is one of the three quay houses: its colonnades and Italian gallery, sculpted pilasters and coffered ceilings rub shoulders with half-timbered houses.

It is not enough for Périgueux to be beautiful; the town is also full of activity. Markets specialised in foie gras every winter, farm-produce markets all year round, jazz concerts in the squares and French song competitions in summer, not forgetting the international ambassadors Mimos, the mime festival, and the culinary book fair or Salon du livre gourmand.

The Place Saint-Louis, in the heart of the preserved sector. Here, terraces bask in the summer sun, but it is transformed into a vast foie gras market twice a week in winter.

The culinary book fair in Périgueux.

Brantôme is a haven of peace, snuggled in greenery encircled by the River Dronne. A mineral ship tied up to the river's blue buckle, the 'Venice of Périgord' is dominated by the Abbey's imposing bell tower, which dates from the Carolingian period.

The Abbey church, renovated in the XIXth century by Abadie, has kept two XIIth-century domes. The convent buildings house a strange museum exhibiting the works of medium Fernand Desmoulin, created during spiritualist séances. The cliff running along the Abbey, punctuated by cavities and shelters, forms a troglodyte circuit. The jewel in its crown is the Last Judgement cave, sculpted into a wall. The walk which follows the river and cliffs to the Renaissance pavilion leads over a curved XVIth century bridge to the peaceful monks' garden. There, from one of the elegant altars, the visitor can appreciate the village tableau that changes with the daylight, sound effects being provided by the mating call of ducks on the river.

Brantôme is inseparable from the River Dronne, which holds the village in a lover's clasp.

Following page - The curved bridge which crosses the river near the Renaissance pavilion and leads to the monks' garden.

The village bears the cultural prints of Pierre de Bourdeilles, alias Brantôme, who built the Château de Richemont on the heights of the village in the XVth century. He withdrew there to write his great work after a life at the Court of France in the train of Catherine de Medicis. The author of Vies des dames galantes sleeps in the chapel crypt, carved with skulls and bones, and the castle is still in his family.

The Côle gurgles under the old bridge covered with pebbles; you could stay here for hours, spend a beautiful day dreaming by the river, if the surrounding landscape didn't call your attention to Saint-Jean-de-Côle. The village is right out of the olden days, and the central marketplace of beaten earth is the perfect viewpoint for the castle, the church and the adjoining corn market.

Previous page - The River Dronne flows along a cliff hollowed out into shelters, paying court to each drowsy watermill it passes.

Back in the XVIth century, Brantôme was abbot at the Benedictine abbey, with its Carolingian tower,

The tall, stocky church, with its single bay, contains the Dordogne's biggest dome: nearly thirteen metres in diameter, which means the base is reinforced by a wooden floor to prevent it from collapsing. The carved capitals tell beautiful but terrible stories: Daniel in the lion's den, the Annunciation... A frieze of fantastic figures runs in a carved garland under the roof of the side chapels.

The massively solid corn market is embedded into one of these chapels, in dazzling osmosis. Standing back, you see the roofs cascading down from the church tower as a hybrid, almost animal vision; a giant stone–and–tile tortoise. The whole village seems to be celebrating its rooftops in an aerial ballet of tiny brown waves, like haloes circling the gilded XIIth to XIVth century residences, some of them half-timbered, in the rue du Fond-du-Bourg.

View from the bridge of Saint-Jean-de-Côle.
Time stands still between ochre stone
and brown roofs.

Following page - The Château de
la Chapelle-Faucher dominates the Côle
with its crenellated tower.

The XVth and XVIth century Château de la Marthonie has two square towers on one side and a round one on the other. A dormer wing from the Renaissance period is built round an arcaded gallery and the main staircase.

The Floralies which lend colour to Saint-Jean-de-Côle in spring are real jewels in the stone. Leaving the village towards Saint-Pierre-de-Côle, the Château de Bruzac looms up on the hillside, freeing its ancient towers from the vegetation that has grown over them, tireless conqueror of a noble past submerged in a rebel landscape.

Previous page – The Château de la Marthonie combines a long classical building and a more austere wing with a Mansart-style pavilion.

The village of La Chapelle-Faucher huddles round the Romanesque church.

Jumilhac-le-Grand is a village magnetised by its castle, best admired from the Place du Foirail. This hairdresser's fantasy cheekily displays its towers in their pointed hats and strangely-shaped rooftops spiked with pepper-pot crowns, tiaras of chimneys and ridgepoles like so many tufts. A clever and prickly delusion of grandeur, inspired by both Gothic and Renaissance styles of architecture.

The Château de Jumilhac has its head full — or almost: go over it with a fine toothcomb for incongruous cherubs and birds, including the ones just passing, which take pleasure in a little teasing and back-combing from their ridgepole perch between two upended quiffs. Visiting these terribly romantic rooftops up in the heights of their glory is like entering a well-dressed headful of crazy dreams.

Renaissance rooftops on the Château de Jumilhac — a festival of toupees and decorated tufts: beauty that'll make your hair stand on end.

In this region where gold was sought, and where a museum in one of the castle's vaulted cellars tells the story of that quest, there is alchemy in the castle gardens: a nocturnal visit during the summer reveals a gold-helmeted silhouette emerging into the luminous enchanted evening. The castle guards the legend of its gentle spinner. In the small chamber, a naive fresco tells the melancholy story of a beauty locked up by her touchy husband. The terraces open onto a view of the Romanesque church and its octagonal tower. At the foot of the castle cliff, the Isle gambols through rocky gorges, still boiling with the energy from its source.

A nocturnal visit to the gardens and the castle rooftops adds to the alchemy distilled by the Musée de l'Or (Gold Museum), installed in the castle basement.

Hautefort is firstly a powerful castle, and can be seen on its hilltop for miles around. The ancient stronghold of the troubadour warrior Bertran de Born was transformed into a castle of classical splendour in the XVIIth century, the vision of the Marquis de Hautefort's architect.

Like a little of the Loire valley escaped into the Dordogne, edged with scrupulously pruned French-style gardens and a majestic wooded park, Hautefort is a castle of tall façades, capped with high slate roofs. Corresponding skylights of the same make can be found on the old hospices in the village below. The surrounding country-side seems to kneel at the feet of this lord, who went up almost entirely in smoke one night in 1968, owing to a badly-extinguished cigarette. Thanks to the tenacity of its owner, the castle managed to rise from its ashes.

Previous page - The visitor can take time to admire the castle from the wooded park and the vast esplanade leading to the drawbridge.

The main courtyard is a perfect balcony for looking at the French-style gardens and Hautefort village.

The village of Saint-Geniès is striking with its unity of ochre buildings, from the phonolite-covered church adjoining the castle to the fine XIIIth and XIVth century residences. Running gently towards the Chironde valley, where many watermills were once exploited, it keeps its revelation for the end, on the edge of the village: the Gothic chapelle du Cheylard has kept its XIVth century frescos illustrating Biblical scenes, rather like a religious comic strip.

On the road to Salignac, Saint-Crépin is a tiny but adorable village worth winkling out for the manoir de la Cipière. This XVIth to XVIIth century manor house with its phonolite-covered roof is accompanied by a polygonal tower.

Gothic chapelle du Cheylard, at Saint-Geniès, containing splendid mural paintings.

Following page - Saint-Geniès village is characterised by its unity, with phonolite-roofed church and castle close by.

Nestling in the hills known here as pechs, the medieval town of Sarlat is divided into two by 'La Traverse' for the Sarladais, rue de la République for the others.

The Place de la Liberté, which hosts the theatre festival each summer, is a real film-set. Sainte-Marie Church has become an unusual covered market, remodelled by Jean Nouvel. Saint-Sacerdos Cathedral stands out from the adjoining architecture, with the cour des Fontaines (Fountain court) and the chapel of the Blue Penitents, the traces of cloisters in the Enfeux garden, the Lantern of the Dead facing its chevet. Just next door is the splendid house of La Boétie, Montaigne's friend, who wrote his *Discours de la servitude volontaire* here.

Previous page
Left - Unimpeded view of the old town
from the pechs.

Right - The Présidial, a tribunal in Henri II's
day, now a restaurant. It is remarkable
for its unusual skylight above a loggia
charmingly swathed in greenery.

La Boétie's house. The ground floor
has the look of an old-fashioned shop-front
and the upper floors wear elegant
Renaissance decoration.

The maze of old cobbled streets hides some surprises for the stroller: the former Présidial with its strange roof, the Hôtel de Gérard full of artists in summer, and all these mansions with their intricately-worked façades topped with heavy phonolite roofs, the Plamon and de Mirandol mansions, Saint Claire's Abbey… The town is dominated by the imposing presence of Saint Joseph's College, formerly a Jesuit temple of knowledge for many years, and providing one of the finest views of Sarlat. The commercial town, which developed from the XIIIth century onwards, has kept its business sense and knows how to attract tourists with its reputation for gastronomy – a reputation often usurped in the summer months. Its architecture, however, is timeless and without artifice. Simply beautiful.

Cobbled alleys and gilded façades.
Sarlat was one of the first towns
to benefit from the loi Malraux

Following page - Sarlat bustles during the
summer months, and then settles into a
quieter rhythm again. The Hôtel de Gérard
is a place where artists meet: there are
many exhibitions of talent in high season.

The Breuil huts at Saint-André-d'Allas are typical of peasant architecture in existence since Gallic times. The stone houses, used as a sheepfold, are perfectly conserved with their high phonolite roofs. Stellio Lorenzi immortalised them in his *Jacquou le Croquant*.

Previous page - The Breuil huts are a fine example of rural architecture.

The cathedral chevet and the enfeux, or arched insets containing a tomb, together make a panorama worth looking at for a long time, before turning to the Lantern of the Dead.

La Roque-Gageac is often flooded by a rise in the Dordogne water level.

The village hurtles down in an ochre waterfall towards the river where it was once a busy port for the merchant gabarres (cargo barges). The embarkation quay now welcomes hordes of tourists for river trips at the foot of the castles: Montfort, Castelnaud, les Milandes... A detour via the village lets the visitor admire the de la Tarde manor that once belonged to a humanist friend of Galileo's and the troglodyte fort which protected the population against invasion, not forgetting the south-facing tropical garden against the cliff, near the church.

Opposite and following page - La Roque-Gageac nestles against the cliff, the better to look at the ribbon of water at its feet.

The Marqueyssac Park, set out on a rocky spur, opens up a 180° panorama of the valley and its castles. The paths snake through the scent of boxwood and from the cliff, the belvedere overhangs la Roque-Gageac, giving an overall view of the village embedded in rock with its halo of green oak forest.

The Château de Beynac, great lord planted on his rock, can be admired from afar. From the village a steep path climbs 150 metres of difference in height, to reach the proud fortress up in the sky. Every stage of the climb reveals an unforgettable view of the river and surrounding houses. Headquarters of one of the Dordogne's four baronies, the Château de Beynac has kept its feudal character, and its owner works tirelessly to restore it while respecting its history. From the phonolite-covered XIIth century chapel, the natural tableau is quite sublime.

Château de Castelnaud, Beynac's historic rival.
It contains a museum of medieval warfare.

Following page - Medieval atmosphere
at Beynac, with its donjon on the defensive
at the edge of the cliff.

Domme appears rather like a mirage, a fortified town suspended between earth and sky on a flight path specially traced for the visitor's imagination. From the esplanade, a terrace giving on to the wide-open landscape with as much fresh air as you like, the river bends round into a loop as if wanting to sweep the whole lot away with it.

The multicoloured geometric pattern of the crops — sunflowers, tobacco, corn, walnuts, hay — strikes the eye. The corn market, the Governor's house and the church make up a postcard picture, coloured by the flower-filled balconies lining the old streets in summer. From here, the town slopes gently down to its monumental gates. The Porte des Tours (Tower Gate) still bears the graffiti traced on its stone in the early XIVth century by Templar prisoners.

Previous page - The Porte des Tours, a mouth under a pointed nose, with two fat cheeks holding in the breath of eternal life.

Domme becomes colourful when spring brings flowers back to the alleys and the open-air market to the square.

Following double spread - The Domme bar, esplanade open to internal transport as well as to strollers, where the eye follows the Dordogne River, escaping over there, off towards the ocean.

Monpazier is the model for fortified towns, marked out with string. Its alleyways cross at right angles, sectioning off the space from the central marketplace and its solidly-built corn market, with the ancient grain measures still intact. All around, nestling against each other, the houses top the covered walkways lined with stalls, opening their arcades and *cornières* (corner openings) towards the light of the marketplace. The rectilinear plan of walled towns such as Monpazier has served as a framework for modern cities: New York and Chicago are directly modelled on this system of blocks, though on a much bigger scale.

Monpazier. A glimpse through the cornières.

*Following page - The Monpazier cornmarket
has kept its ancient grain measures,
and hosts a lot of summer events.*

This XIIIth century fortified town has kept three of its six original gates, which closed off access. It also keeps alive the memory of one of its 'enfants terribles', the novelist and adventurer Jean Galmot, who died in 1928 in Guyana, where he had gone to make his fortune.

Belvès seems to be embedded in the landscape. Its shape can be made out little by little, on approaching; a crown of seven towers, steeples and belfries sticking up here and there, perched up high on the hillside. The Place des Armes with its XVth century corn market, and the beautiful surrounding residences, have kept all their medieval charm. Urval has preserved its XIIIth-XIVth century communal oven, which, together with the Romanesque church and its belfry, gives a timeless vision of the village.

Previous page - The covered walkways suggest a stroll around the central square.

Belvès, with its towers and campaniles, clings to the hills and looks out over the valley towards infinity.

The Cistercian abbey at Cadouin flushes crimson when the last of the sun caresses its great golden body: the walker, diminished by its sober majesty, steps back further to take in the whole vision, with the grain market in the foreground and the convent buildings. Processions of pilgrims came through here from the XIIth century onwards, until the authenticity of the shroud thought to be Christ's was contested in 1934.

The cloister contains many beautiful scenes; sacred and profane mingle, as do flamboyant Gothic and Renaissance architecture.

Cadouin village seems to kneel in homage before the sober façade of the abbey church. Only the corn market tries to rival so much beauty.

Saint-Avit-Sénieur Abbey is to benefit from a restoration project. The presbytery hosts exhibitions.

Following page - Cistercian, elegant imposing, Cadouin Abbey drew many pilgrimages when it contained what was believed to be the Holy Shroud.

The church of Saint-Avit-Sénieur rises like a fortress near the Couze valley. One of its two towers, destroyed by the passage of time, gives it the look of a ghost ship washed up in the greenery. The abbey church and the former presbytery have just been dazzlingly restored, and the geometric frescos in the nave are surprisingly modern.

The church of Saint-Avit-Sénieur rises like a fortress near the Couze valley. One of its two towers, destroyed by the passage of time, gives it the look of a ghost ship washed up in the greenery. The abbey church and the former presbytery have just been dazzlingly restored, and the geometric frescos in the nave are surprisingly modern.

Molières is one of those little fortified towns with which you fall hopelessly in love at first sight. The central marketplace with its porch, the imposing church and further away, the remains of the castle; the fine houses carefully renovated, give it an old-fashioned charm that lingers on afterwards.

At the confluence of the Vézère and the Dordogne, Limeuil looks on at the mingling of the waters as it has always done. The village has attracted several artists and craftsmen, who keep the doors of their workshops open. A wander through the alleys up to the top of the village leads to the castle arboretum, overlooking the valley and the pebble beaches where tourists sunbathe. Outside the village slumbers the well-proportioned Romanesque chapel of Saint-Martin. In the countryside, a garden museum offers a fascinating trip through humanity's plant heritage.

The walled village of Molières, as pretty as a picture with its central marketplace and its imposing church which can be seen from afar.

Following page - The waters of the Vézère and the Dordogne meet at Limeuil, attractive confluence with its two bridges at right angles.

Bergerac owes its cultural and economic development to a curious historic mixture of influences: the Dordogne River, its vines and Protestantism.

The wine market was already flourishing when the town became Huguenot, exporting its Monbazillac to Protestant Holland, by means of the Dordogne's current leading directly to Bordeaux and the ocean. The Récollets cloister, headquarters of the Inter-professional Council of Wines of the Bergerac region, tells the story of the vine and initiates the palate into wine-tasting. In the Place du Feu, the Tobacco Museum follows the history of those plantations which made the fortunes of the Dordogne valley farmers. The old town, beautifully renovated, is sprinkled with half-timbered houses, better admired from the other bank.

The church of Saint-Jacques and the Place Pelissière make up one of the most beautiful perspectives in the old town of Bergerac.

Following page - For many years, the banks of the Dordogne earned their living by trading with the gabarre barges, bringing produce from the high country down to the port at Bordeaux.

Near the church of Montcaret lie the remains of a Gallo-Roman villa, arranged around an interior courtyard and a swimming-pool decorated with mosaics on an aquatic theme.

The Château de Saint-Michel-de-Montaigne is above all a place of memory: Montaigne's tower contains the author of the Essais' library intact, with his maxims written on the ceiling. A kind of summary of the Dordogne's humanist soul, in a sense.

Montaigne's library tower in which he wrote is rather like a concentration of humanism, due to the author's maxims that the famous philosopher had inscribed on the beams.

Following page – The renovation of Bergerac's old quarters shows off the fine houses near the River Dordogne.

Countryside

The Dordogne's size is as impressive as its history: 100 km east-west, 100 km north-south for almost 9 200 sq km. It is the third French department in terms of size, after the Landes and the Gironde, and the scenery is varied: a ramble in the Auvézère gorges looks very like the steep paths of the Massif Central, and a trip into the vineyards around Bergerac calls to mind the neighbourhood of Bordeaux. From one to the other, a world full of opposites that attract and false similarities, one unique journey made up of diverse colours, shapes and soils.

Previous page - In the Dordogne,
there is always a little path leading
to the middle of nowhere to get lost on.

The Dordogne has a fertile soil, and has
inherited a long tradition of mixed farming.

The steep contours and the rocky paths of the higher part of the Dordogne make up a rather wild landscape of woods and prairies. The natural curiosity known as the *Puy des âges*, a shale notch haloed with deep purple heather splits the green horizon so the eye can see further, right to the borders of Limousin.

The rivers springing up here are still streams and waterfalls just escaped from the Auvergne mountains: the Isle, the Loue and the Auvézère serve as clear springboards for daring kayakists, bouncing up at Saut-Ruban or the Blâme waterfall. In the Dordogne highlands, ever since the early Middle Ages, the cold waters of the Bandiat have tempered Nontron knife blades – these are among the oldest clasp knives in France.

Walk through the scents, colours and gentle rustlings of the forest for real communion with nature.

Following page - Woods and lakes are the main features of the Dordogne highlands.

The rivers Côle and Dronne, joining up on their way to the Charente, used to work a little fleet of watermills with their current, which becomes rather turbulent at the Chalard falls.

Over to the west, the waters flow more calmly into two huge ponds, Saint-Estèphe and Jemaye, ideal for boating and lined with guingettes (open-air cafés) during the summer. The stream becomes languid and even bogged-down in the Double forest, former swamp drained by the Trappist monks of Echourgnac in the XIXth century.

These tormented landscapes inspired Eugène le Roy's novel *l'Ennemi de la mort* (Death's Enemy). He added a play to his work, largely devoted to peasant conditions: 'An unspeakable melancholy was felt in that desolate region (...), kingdom of fever'*. This fetid corner of the Dordogne has been transformed into a paradise for shooting and fishing, between marshland and the haunts of woodpigeons.

* Extract from l'Ennemi de la Mort, *quoted in* Eugène Le Roy (1836-1907) *by Joëlle Chevé, éditions Sud Ouest.*

Previous page - The Double, land of drained marshes, is more mysterious than ever when the dawn mists rise over the ponds.

The Dronne house evokes the history of this wild region, marked by the watermills one by one along the river.

The Dordogne valley, wide and fertile, flows from the cliffs of black Périgord to the Bergerac vineyards, passing through the limpid cingles (horseshoe-shaped river bends) of Trémolat and Domme. Henry Miller spent a month at Trémolat, the epicentre from which he wove his passion for the whole of the Dordogne, described in *The Colossus of Maroussi* 'Nothing can stop me from believing that Cro-Magnon man settled here because he was extremely intelligent with a highly-developed sense of beauty'*.

From the Domme esplanade, the river's blue loop links the colourful crops that it fertilizes: blood-brown tobacco, once typical of this landscape, now disappearing as a result of European directives; blonde corn, rape and sunflower furrows; the dotted lines of walnut trees...

Extract from The Colossus of Maroussi, *quoted in* L'invention d'un paradis, le Périgord, *by Chantal Tanet and Tristan Hordé, Editions Fanlac.*

The countryside is starred with dovecotes, turrets, small shelters and barns: a whole rural heritage to protect.

Tobacco, grown for years in the Dordogne valley, is dried in well-ventilated wooden huts.

Following page - At a bend in the path, a dry-stone hut bears witness to ancient skills.

The painter and writer François Augiéras withdrew into a cave at the end of the cliff path, looking on to the changing landscape from just the right spot on the river. This 'Western barbarian' was an insatiable traveller, who made an interior voyage on the banks of the Dordogne. This is what he wrote at Carsac-Aillac, just before the waters quietened: 'Downstream, the Dordogne passes in torrents under huge rocky cliffs: a region of rapids, split up by islands, gravel and sand banks, an absolutely virgin territory (...) Clear water leaping up from the pebbles, live water. A powerful murmur, a scent of water flowing fast under the overhanging cliffs. You feel you are on the banks of the Ganges where it leaves the Himalayas!"*

*Letters to Paul Placet, Editions Fanlac.

Previous page - The crops have fun drawing geometric figures.

Every evening, the twilight mood finds a renewed landscape, neither exactly the same nor completely different...

Bright yellow sunflowers and rapeseed light up the scene: a touch of sunshine at ground level.

The valley is now a tourist site, but it has remained faithful to the peasants who shaped it. The gabarres which formerly transported the wood needed by the vineyard coopers have made way for boatloads of tourists curious to observe the scenery on the other side of the river, surprised to see the elegant castle of Montfort approaching, or leaning back the better to see the cliff at la Roque-Gageac.

The Céou refreshes a wild and rocky valley then, after a foray into Quercy, gets lost in the river which sweeps it up at Castelnaud. The Dordogne and the Vézère meet up at Limeuil, dream confluence whose pebble beach attracts sunbathers in the summer months.

Exuberant plant life and clear water, ideal spot for a refreshing descent in a canoe.

Following page - The harvest arrives with the first summer days, rolling golden balls on the bronzed back of the land.

Autumn arrives with its reddish current, swelling the trickle of water along which the canoes slip in summer. The Vézère, in which Cro-Magnon man bathed so long ago, has bitten into the cliff, opening up great hole-like shelters under the rock which were occupied from prehistoric times to the Renaissance and even again in the sixties by farmers.

It is surely not by chance that a group of Buddhist centres was set up in the seventies on the Jor slopes. The monks, exiled from a Tibet sacrificed to China, were invited by a generous donor to pursue their pacifist combat here. The stupa, coloured mats and prayer wheels found their place on the top of this hill reaching up to infinity, just above the valley of the first men.

Previous page - Colours that dazzle the eye on a horizon in perpetual motion.

Dardé's famous statue 'Primitive Man' stands near the National Prehistory Museum at Les Eyzies.

The Vézère meanders gracefully, seen from the Jor slopes.

Land of origins, conducive to meditation, this spiritual perimeter represents the universal for some, or simply a picture of unrivalled beauty and a chance to commune with nature for others. The paragliders taking off from here can touch eternity, but the dazzled spectators, frozen on the edge of space, merely dream of it.

The causses revive certain traditions: truffles, like at Sorges, or vines — wiped out by phylloxera — such as the Domme wine, remade in the Céou valley. Yet the great Dordogne vineyards which have always existed stretch out next to those of Bordeaux: the Bergerac wines comprise 13 appellations. The most famous, monbazillac, made the fortunes of local traders who exported this sweet white wine in Europe from the XVth century.

Plazac is a lively village, concerned with spiritual horizons and the quality of life.

From the troglodyte village La Madeleine there is a view of the Vézère valley. The paleolithic deposit discovered on the site has given its name to the Magdalenian era.

Following page - The rows of vines zigzag through the Bergerac landscape.

The XVIth century castle proudly dominates a horizon of vines made up of so many lines running down the valley, turning from green to purple before the grape harvest. The secret alchemy of morning mists and warm autumn sunshine develops the famous 'noble rottenness' needed for monbazillac. That voluptuous celebration from vine to wine enchants the neighbourhood at local fairs where everyone drinks to the future millesime.

From Monbazillac, the eye can see
far across the vineyards towards
Bergerac and the Dordogne valley.

Everything in the Dordogne is part of a hymn to the countryside, to the farmed lands and breeding prairies, yet the forest swallows up the landscape, of which it makes up almost half, closing off viewpoints with its various oaks, chestnuts and conifers. A few dark forests, escaped from the terrible storm of 1999, still seem to shelter a Jacquou strayed out of the XIXth century: the Brade forest near Montignac where Eugène le Roy's Croquant was born, the Bessède forest between vineyards and walled towns and the Double forest, pitted with ponds and marshes.

Each has its personality, its woodland, its game, its treasures... The ceps stick up their round heads as soon as the damp earth feels the earliest and latest sunshine of the year: spring and autumn celebrate the mushroom.

Vines and wine. Cultivating,
in every sense of the word.

Like the farmed land, the bouquet of gardens flourishing in the Dordogne reflects the domestic part of the countryside. Each of these small earthly paradises embodies the soul of its creator: well-disciplined French-style gardens at the Château de Hautefort and the Manoir d'Eyrignac; English gardens carefully dishevelled by Sardy at Vélines, with terraces and lakes; rural ambience at l'Albarède; humanity interpreted through plants, or the history of cultures in both senses of the word, at Limeuil; water gardens at Carsac, between streams and waterfalls; collections of bamboos and grasses at Buisson; a garden of imagination peopled with myths and legends at Terrasson... and so many other ephemeral splendours, moving, and changing with the seasons.

Previous page - In the misty dawn light, the water contours melt into the banks, and mysterious shapes emerge.

Shooting and fishing are traditional practices in the Dordogne, way of life for some, licence to kill for the others: the opening of the season is a highly-charged moment of the year for both.

Rural architecture grows out of the quality of the soil, rich or poor: white stone in the Ribéracois, ochre walls in the Dordogne valley and slates on the Limousin border. The flat phonolite stones are assembled together, weighing a ton on the roofs of individual mansions in the Sarladais built from that limestone which links cliffs with buildings in the region.

In the Double, the landscape was all marshland and forests, so for many years local builders had to make do with these fragile raw materials, and the houses were built of cob. The Parcot farm retraces the history of this kind of building for visitors. Further away, the Vendoire peat bogs explain the surrounding ecosystem, and how fuel was found in the soil.

The granaries built on piles protect the cereal harvest from rodents.

Following page - An ocean of mist wraps round the Dordogne riverbed like a cosy eiderdown thrown down from Castelnaud.

There is also underground scenery, for the depths of the Dordogne hold a wealth of grottos, chasms and caves, galleries and natural cavities known as cluzeaux. The Proumeyssac chasm at Bugue is a crystal cathedral, a witness to the work of land and time which together created this geological fairyland of translucent stalagmites and stalactites. Not far from there, at Buisson, the Maxange caves, opened in 2003, reveal a composition of the same eccentric transparency.

In the Villars cave, in the north of the department, natural concretions have blended with the 17 000-year-old prehistoric paintings, including the famous blue horse, to work a joint metamorphosis.

Natural cavities, quarries, caves and shelters under the rock, some of which show signs of ancient human occupation, hollow out the Dordogne substratum.

The Blue Horse, famous prehistoric painting in the Villars cave, dates back 17 000 years.

Following page - A light veil seems to be trying to unite earth and sky in this soft morning atmosphere.

The Dordogne is a very human land, and at the same time a region of landscapes: natural spaces chiselled out by time; Technicolour exteriors modelled by human hands with strength and genius – with pain too, bending double under the weight of history. Reading these land-scapes is like coming back to your roots, to the earth's womb.

You find yourself hoping to see one of our far-off ancestors emerge from the hole-pitted cliffs of the Vézère banks, come to tell us more about what we imagine on the basis of a few bones or drawings on a cave wall.

'When I am in the Dordogne, I unders-tand why Man chose to create Art there more than 30 000 years ago, for here, even nature is talented' wrote Georges Bataille. There is nothing astonishing in fact that these life-size stage-sets and live impressionist tableaux continue to inspire artists of all kinds: painters, writers, filmmakers and musicians pool their influences in a symphony of shapes and colours whose echo carries far beyond the Dordogne.

Previous page - Staggering sunset in the Dordogne.

The cliffs and the River Vézère, unchanging couple from the Valley of Man, now part of the Unesco World Heritage.

Gastronomy

Land of gastronomy, the Dordogne can flatter itself that it produces culinary treasures and makes good use of them. The many farm-produce markets flourishing in towns and villages overflow with fresh foodstuffs, often rare, like the varieties of fruit and vegetables dying out.

The colours and tastes change with the seasons: first ceps and early strawberries, late vine peaches...The marchés de gras, markets specialised in foie gras and other duck and goose products warm up the winter with their convivial ambience; carcasses and roasted chestnuts are handed out to all and sundry, liver carefully chosen for a tender burial in a terrine.

Previous page - Whatever the generation, women's cooking is full of personal recipes made from local products.

The Périgueux market on the Place de la Clautre and the Place du Coderc is the countryside come to town, to paraphrase Alphonse Allais.

The Dordogne is a huge garden, a lush Eden where it would be in bad taste not to give in to temptation. The table is always set; the simplest things satisfy the famished and revive a jaded palate: bread golden from the wood-burning oven, a walnut on goat's cheese, a glass of pécharmant wine, and the passing townie is transformed into an authentic native son.

Both traditional and organic market gardeners bring strangely but deliciously shaped produce to their stalls, not really graded for mass marketing!

Following page - At Villefranche-du-Périgord, there is a Chestnut Museum, dedicated to the conker that crunches under your feet in the woods, and the roasting chestnuts wreathed in woodsmoke, warming the first frosts.

Family recipes came out of drawers to find a place on the menus of the farmhouse-inns, which came into being as agriculture was opening up to tourism: tourrain, soup made with duck fat, onions, garlic and optional tomato; mique, a kind of dumpling; duck breasts with Sarladaise potatoes (fried in the duck fat) and the tourtière, or meat pie, with salsify are enough for the biggest appetite. In the winter mists, the pig is still killed by some, who insist on preparing themselves the *cochonnailles,* or pork products: black and white puddings, hams and pâtés that will last all year.

Previous page - Every meeting in the Dordogne is a feast.

Little pigs get bigger and more appetising. The day of the killing arrives in this farmyard, with an early-morning sacrifice in the coldest hours of winter to prepare the cochonnailles *that will feed a whole year of feasting.*

The cep sticks up its round hat, sought-after in the damp forests warmed by early sunshine: walkers get lost in the clearings, hoping secretly to take home a few ceps in their baskets.

Autumn is the season of abundance, and tons of ceps are expertly negotiated in the covered market at Villefranche-du-Périgord. Private customers, who will bottle them up, and restaurant owners hurrying to serve them in omelettes, besiege this Mecca of transaction. A few steps away is a museum devoted to the cep, but it does not really explain the magic link between this forest-dweller and its environment.

Above and following page - The cep in season drives everyone into action: this fine boletus mushroom has all the Dordogne at its feet. Its incomparable flavour will end up in a jar, a fricassee or an omelette.

The truffle, Dordogne's 'black diamond', has become rare in only a century. The *tuber melano-sporum*, which remains on the causses, is worth more as a result. The current price is fixed at Sainte-Alvère market. The eco- museum and the truffle-hunters' path at Sorges explain the truffle's mysterious alchemy, one soil and one tree, and the different ways of unearthing it, with a dog or by raising the flies that lay their eggs on it.

While humans try to domesticate it, the truffle prefers to hide in the wild, with burnt earth as the only sign of its presence. A touch of 'melano' transfigures a pâté or scrambled eggs, and its scent alone embalms the eggs intended for an omelette without the tiniest slice of truffle ever touching the omelette itself. At the *Auberge de la Truffe* at Sorges, Pierre Corre has to stop himself adding a black soupçon to all his recipes: the address is a must for those wanting to taste the precious tuber.

*The art of unearthing truffles
is not for everyone: first train your dog,
and then know where to look...*

*Following page - The black diamond
is as pricey as gold dust, but a mere touch
is enough to transform a simple omelette
into unforgettable gastronomy.*

Everything is edible in the fat duck, and especially the liver. This is also the case in its friend the goose, more expensive for the consumer owing to its subtler flavour, but preferred by fans to the duck's stronger taste.

The liver, obtained by force-feeding the birds intensively, is a golden colour when it arrives on festive tables, having been cooked in a pan or in salt, or partially-cooked, in a terrine.

The art of making foie-gras can be learnt during theme weekends in farmhouse-inns or traditional hotels: you buy your liver at a *marché de gras*, you learn to prepare it and cook it, then you take away your delicious trophy, ready to impress your friends. 'I made it myself in the Dordogne!' The signature of quality and know-how.

Previous page - The free-range geese and ducks are generously force-fed, and at the end of the day, supply a foie gras to eat pan-cooked, partially-cooked or tinned.

There are lots of marchés de gras *in the Dordogne. From autumn to spring, there are several prize markets in Périgueux, run by culinary associations or* confréries, *notably the 'Pâté de Périgueux' brotherhood.*

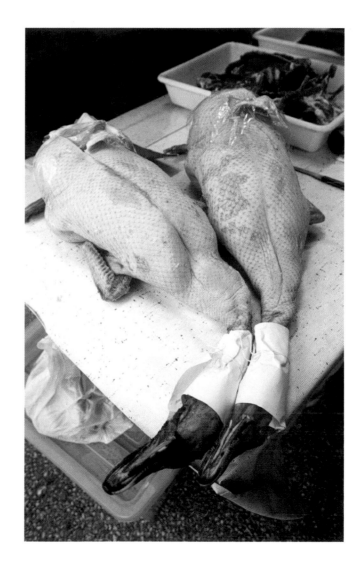

The walnut trees are a traditional part of the landscape, especially in the 'black country'. The walnut used to blacken the fingers of the nutshellers, paid by the kilo of shelled fruit: the husk was removed and the shell broken in half to extract the kernels, by tapping them on a flat stone placed across the knees. Walnuts have always had a special place on the Dordogne table: even Cro-Magnon man nibbled them 17 000 years ago. They are known by several local names, and their flavour enhances cakes, wines, oil, and aperitif nibbles, fresh, in kernels or dried.

The walnut is traditional in the Dordogne, especially in Quercy, where walnut plantations are part of the landscape and a few mills still produce their own walnut oil.

Following page - Land of plenty and diversity, the Dordogne is a feast for the eyes and the taste buds.

Strawberries made the Dordogne's fortune, both the gariguette, and the wild variety, the woodland mara, before retreating a little from the advance of their Spanish neighbours. The Vergt region is striped with clear tarpaulins under which rows of strawberry plants soak up the first hot weather, so as to deliver their fruit to the local and national markets.

The first strawberries to brighten the stalls announce the arrival of spring. At the end of the season, the fields are open to fruit-picking for jam-making. The strawberry suits a variety of desserts: sorbet, tarts and melbas; in its natural form it is impossible to resist on your way home

Previous page - The strawberry flourished in the seventies under the plastic tunnels at Vergt: the Dordogne markets like the small gariguette and the wild mara des bois varieties best.

Nature hangs on to life until it is exhausted.

from the market...

The Bergerac vineyards, already mentioned in the XIIIth century, were a great commercial success in the XVIIth and XVIIIth centuries. Thirteen appellations rub shoulders on the 12 400 hectares of vineyard; the most famous are still monbazillac among the dessert wines and pécharmant for the reds, although the mellow de saussignac wines are now making an impression. The Inter-professional Council of Wines of the Bergerac region offers wine-tasting sessions where amateurs can compare these wines with those from other soils, learn to define their sensations, develop their œnological vocabulary and co-ordinate eye, nose and mouth.

Dry white, sweet, rosé or red:
Bergerac wines have the colours
to suit all tastes.

Following page - Rows of vines,
low-angled shadows and peaceful
sheep paint an elegant landscape.

The home distillers who roam the countryside in the cold and the steam from their stills are becoming rare. They are disappearing, as are the individuals bringing their fruit to be converted into plum or pear brandy.

And so the home distillers are now working for those who've forgotten the tradition: Clovis Reymond at Villamblard, one of the oldest, has been distilling since 1834. The spirits — fruit in brandy, aperitifs and liqueurs — are packaged in bottles reeking of history.

Previous page - In the chilly dawn, the home-distiller settles in a lonely corner of the countryside to distil the fruits of his passion: pears, plums and others...

A walk in the Dordogne brings together various pleasures: the peace and quiet of a small village, a surprising viewpoint, a castle's turbulent history, gentle natural scenery, meeting warm and genuine people and, last but not least, the delicious spread of a table open to all.

Portraits of France[©]

Burgundy
Brittany
Dordogne

French Riviera
Paris
Provence

... and more than 40 books in French on the towns and regions of France.
Consult our website **www.declics.fr**

© **Editions Déclics 2004**
14, rue des Volontaires - 75015 Paris - France
Tél. 33 (1) 53 69 70 00 - **Fax** 33 (1) 42 73 15 24.
E-mail : *contact@declics.fr*

Printed by Corlet, Condé-sur-Noireau (14)
France N° 77122

Dépôt légal 2nd quarter 2004
Code ISBN 2-84768-061-6
Code Sodis 9876590

www.declics.fr

*Following double spread - Powerful outline
of the Château de Beynac as daylight fades.
Beynac was one of the four Périgord baronies,
along with Bourdeilles, Biron and Mareuil.*

*On back cover - Mother Nature puts on a show.
It's beautiful; it's the Dordogne.*